Copyright@2022 Emmanuel and Zoey

Johnson All Rights Reserved

ISBN: 978-1-66786-558-4

A Love Letter to My Dad

Dedication

We dedicate this book in memory of our father Travous Johnson. We miss you so much. We have decided to put it in writing.

Dear Dad,

Today is Saturday March 5, 2022 and I'm thinking about the times you would hug me. You would always tell me I was smart.

Dear Dad,

Today I'm sad because it is my awards day, and you are not here. I could remember you always being at all my award shows. I'm glad mom was able to make it.

<u>What do you miss about your loved one?</u>

Today mom cooked gumbo. Her gumbo was good. Her gumbo wasn't better than yours. Your gumbo was the best.

Dad with his
Chef hat. Dad
loved to cook.

What was your loved ones best cooked dish? What did you love about it?

Today we are grocery shopping. I miss you holding my hand in the store. I miss you taken me to movies and purchasing extra butter for the popcorn.

Where was your favorite places to spend time with your loved one?

Sometimes I get sad and cry

When I'm sad and cry I talk to my mom and uncles. Talking to my loved ones help me to know they care. Talking about why I'm sad helps relieve my hurt.

Who is your support system?

How do you cope with loosing someone? Do you have someone to share your memories?

Dad we know you are gone, but not forgotten. You will always be in our hearts. The memories of your bright smile, tasty food, and play time will always be in our hearts. We will always love you.

We have created a journal for you to write the good times and how you feel from losing a loved one. We hope this book has been of good help to you.

<u>Your Day 1 Journal</u>

<u>Your Day 2 Journal</u>

<u>Your Day 3 Journal</u>

<u>Your Day 4 Journal</u>

<u>Your Day 5 Journal</u>

<u>Your Day 6 Journal</u>

Has writing your own journal help you with grieving? If so how?

Zoey and I hope by sharing our memories has helped you. If so, please share on the next page.

<u>Share your thoughts</u>

The End!